Spiritual Foods for Senior Saints

Devotions for 80 Years and Beyond

May you be filled with the love of God.
Psalm 34

Patt Devitt

by

Patt M. Devitt

authorHOUSE®

AuthorHouse™
1663 Liberty Drive
Bloomington, IN 47403
www.authorhouse.com
Phone: 1 (800) 839-8640

Published by AuthorHouse 11/08/2016

ISBN: 978-1-5246-4571-7 (sc)
ISBN: 978-1-5246-4569-4 (hc)
ISBN: 978-1-5246-4570-0 (e)

Library of Congress Control Number: 2016917332

Print information available on the last page.

This book is printed on acid-free paper.

Acknowledgements

This book came to be because of the cheerleader enthusiasm, the artistic eye, the unrelenting encouragement, the proofing reading ability, and the guidance of these special people: Suzy Telford, D'Ann Gunn, Fleta Edwards, Dr. Helen DeBevoise, Dr. Caroline Brown, Aileen Henderson, and Carolyn Ezell. Thank you.

Thanks, too, to Charles Edwards, Ann Weston, and the staff of Capstone Village who helped me navigate in the computer world.

Contents

Introduction

Dear Reader,

From my lofty age of 85 I find the decade of the eighties presenting some unique challenges I did not face in the teen years, middle years, or even retirement years. My body is different (demanding more maintenance, more care), my thinking is different (short term getting shorter, recalling people's names getting harder), and my social patterns are different (energy and hearing levels make being in large gatherings uncomfortable). Therefore, smaller groups of friends are my community of choice. This time of life has been gifted to me. It's like God is giving me an invitation to another way of life. He still wants me to laugh, love and learn, just in a different lifestyle than I've had before. This change naturally brings out anxieties and discomfort; however, He also has provided a way for me to realize His lifestyle for me if I follow His lead. God's dream for us is much greater than we could dream for ourselves. E. M. Forester says, "We must be willing to let go the life we have planned, so we can have the life that is waiting for us."

I think of entering the eighth decade like entering a store with the widest selection of lifestyles. This store has a manager: God. He decides the store's hours, when to open and when to

close. He has also sent His top salesman – The Holy Spirit --
to show me the best selections tailored to fit my needs. I have
a choice of accepting these suggestions – for that is what they
are, suggestions – or not. I am capable of making other choices,
because some of the suggestions made by this salesman I may find
too strange or off-the-wall. However, if I do listen to and take
the advice of this super salesman, I know I will find joy, peace,
patience, kindness, faithfulness, gentleness, and self-control.

Here are thirty-one devotions exploring what the Bible has
to say with the issues I am facing in my eighty -year. I've written
only thirty-one and included some blank pages in hopes, dear
Reader, that you will continue writing your own thoughts as
you read bible passages and think about your relationship with
our Lord.

Resting

"So the people rested on the seventh day."

Exodus 16: 22-30

I heaved myself out of bed this morning, put both feet on the floor, made coffee and read the paper, took a shower, dressed and wanted to go back to bed. My body says will this be another 'slow day.' But before I fret and fume about not being able to do everything for everyone else all the time, I need to acknowledge the reality of my situation and accept myself exactly as I am today – with an aging body that needs more rest – saying with Katherine de Schlegel, "Be still, my soul: The Lord is on thy side." The Bible, in several places, says the Lord emphasizes the need for rest as His people. He knows we can't be on the go 24/7, especially in our elderly years. He sets us an example. The least I can do is to return this sentiment by admitting I am what I am and what I am is wonderful. And to take care of this aging body with gratitude.

So when I have a 'slow day' – days I need to catch up on my rest – I will pamper myself with simple things. I might have an extra nap or paint my toenails green instead of red or watch a favorite video. Or I might do nothing, have a quiet time with an extra cup of decaf on the balcony watching the Lord's world unfold. It's a day of renewal. Today I need to be there for myself.

Thank you, Lord, for loving me and through the Holy Spirit and scripture teaching me how to take care of this body you gifted me. Help me learn how to join you in your sustaining rest. In Jesus name I pray. Amen.

Reflection

Going Toward the Unknown

"Answer my when I call, O God of my righteousness!
You have given me relief when I was in distress, be
gracious to me and hear my prayer."

Psalm 4

As I journey into the elderly years I need more than ever to know
that the Lord is with me. The unknown is dark and scary to me.
Darkness hides all sorts of potentially harmful things: ferocious
animals (health and financial snares), venous snakes (uncaring
health care people and loss of ability to care for myself), lurking
enemies (changes I don't want). Any could be waiting just out
of sight. That's the trouble with the unknown – you just don't
know what's waiting there. A couple of wrong moves could
bring disaster.

In the words of Psalm 4 I hear words to still my anxious heart.
When I ask God to have mercy and hear my prayer, He does.

As a faithful follower of Christ, God will 'take personal care' of me, counseling and guiding me about dangers I might overlook. He will make known to me His will through the Comforter and be with me as I face the challenges of growing older every day. I have reason to be apprehensive but when I am in the right relationship with God I need not fear. I will do my part: laugh, love and learn something new every day.

Dear Heavenly Father, may I ever seek to know your will for me trusting You will provide for me. Amen.

Reflection

Freedom

"If ye continue in my word, then are ye my
disciples indeed; And you shall know the truth,
and the truth shall make you free."

John 8:32

My daughter visited us at the beach for a few days without her
family. When she was leaving she said, "You know, Mom, you
have the best of all worlds! You have congenial people living
around you that you may visit when you want, yet you have the
privacy of your home when you want. You and Vince eat meals
in a restaurant or cook at home – and go to a movie when you
like. My goodness, such freedom!"

I never thought of being older in years and being 'free' in the
same context but she is right. During this time I am grateful to
get to write my own script for living each day which is a delicious
type of freedom.

Another type of freedom, a more lasting one, is what John records. It comes when I gratefully recognize the number of ways the Lord has intervened in my daily life creating in me a feeling of wonder, certainty, gratitude, and freedom from depression, disappointment and disenchantment. It allows me to walk securely and 'free' each of my days no matter how few or many, sure in the awesome knowledge that as a follower of Jesus Christ my life is in the finest hands.

I know I will not live forever – nor do I want to. But, I don't want to waste my time lamenting the things I cannot do or worrying about the things of tomorrow. While I am here I want the type of joy, freedom, and knowing the truth that being a disciple of Christ brings. And, if I choose, I'll eat my dessert first tonight.

May I continue learning Your word, most gracious and loving Father, as I journey through my elderly years. I thank You for this day which you have made. May I rejoice and be glad in it. Amen.

Reflection

I am known

"For thou didst form my inward parts, thou didst
knit me together in my mother's womb. I praise
thee, for thou art fearfully and wonderfully made.
Wonderful are thy works! Thou knowest me quite
well: my frame is not hid from thee."

Psalm 139:13-14

I gratefully accept that the Lord created me for a purpose – He
knew what I would look like, what my abilities are, what my
personality would be like. I believe and am awed by the wonder
that I was gifted (or made) for the special purpose the Lord has
in mind for my life. In my advanced years, I struggle sometimes
to know how to carry out those special purposes, although I do
not doubt that they are there. I do think that I have not used
His gifts to the fullest extent nor always followed His ways and
when I worry about these things I take comfort in the fact that
this is why Jesus came into this world in the form of a man: to
intercede for me.

For all the ups and the downs of my life I thank Him for His loving wisdom in allowing the things that have influenced me, that have allowed me to be open, to respond to His guidance. If things had been different I would not be the person I am.

Accepting that I am "wonderfully made" means knowing that the Lord is not the least bit dissatisfied with my inborn talents, intelligence, appearance, personality. He has plans to use these things to further His kingdom on earth. Therefore, I am one of a kind, an original—uniquely designed.

Dear Lord, I am in awe of You as Maker of the Universe and of mankind. You chose me for one of your missions. I kneel in worship before such a loving power. Amen.

Reflection

Overwhelmed

"Come to me, all you that are weary and carry heavy burdens, and I will give you rest."

Matthew 11: 28 – 30

There are times when I desperately seek help. Times when the 'what ifs' and the 'and thens' overwhelm me: the terror of facing the threat of a life threatening illness, chemotherapy treatments, finding I may have some pending financial disaster (paying for a root canal or filling an expensive medical prescription), the death of a spouse or friend, or some major life decisions (moving to a retirement facility or nursing facility). It could be an accumulation of smaller things: my washing machine is leaking; the toilet keeps running; I've lost my helper's phone (or cell) number; I can't find one of my hearing aids and I don't have any new batteries. The stress brought on by these and other life situations cannot be solved by taking a nap. And when friends quote the old, much used phrase, "God never gives you more than you can handle," I wonder.

I wonder if facing such condition is not a God-time prompt, a reminder of the peace and comfort such a contact with Him can bring. He is always there watching as I experience stress trials, even personal conflicts. I cannot believe my experiencing stress is about testing or punishing me, rather, it's about using this opportunity to remind me of His promises, strengthening my faith. He promises to help me when I face difficulties and to share my burden. This does not mean He will hand me answers or make my anxiety disappear. Rather, He will show me the tools I need to handle my "impossible" situations. Exercising my faith, I can rest in the knowledge that Jesus and my family of faith can help me when I face my struggles.

Lord, thank You that Your place of rest has always been with us. Thank you for showing me the tools I need to handle my struggles when I confess them. In Jesus name I pray. Amen.

Reflection

Broken heart

"The Lord is near to the brokenhearted and saves
the crushed in spirit."

Psalm 34: 17 – 20

I have experienced times of the deep valley of sadness, but also
times of mountain top joy. When I feel my heart is breaking –
the death of a friend (human or animal), death of a spouse, a
mandatory change of lifestyle – I look to prayer and scripture as
well as friends for help. It's comforting to know that the Lord is
close by as I navigate through the grieving process.

Through prayer I will make known to the Lord my anxious,
troubled heart and ask for His guidance. I can only do this if I
am willing to commit to listening for and willing to follow the
leadership of the Holy Spirit. I am told that "when the righteous
cry out, the Lord listens; he delivers them from all their troubles."

*God, remind me in my suffering that Your love endures. Guide
me now into a life of greater faith and service. Amen.*

Patt M. Devitt

Reflection

Lonely

"If any off you lacks wisdom, let him ask God, who gives generously to all without reproach, and it will be given him. But let him ask in faith, without doubting, for one who doubts is like a wave of the sea that is driven and tossed by the wind."

James 1:2-5

It's a real challenge for me not to feel left behind when the loneliness blues descend. I know that my family and others care for me, but they have lifestyles that can't include me always. I cannot expect them to always be at my beck and call, so I need advice on how to handle this situation before it gets to the pity-party stage. James says God has a 'bountiful supply' of wisdom for all who *openly* ask for and expect an answer. No one ever promised me a life without its challenges, difficulties or temptations! Rather, I am granted times to lean on the Lord and learn the wisdom he teaches. In verse 8 James also warns me, "If you don't ask with faith, don't expect the Lord to give you any solid answer."

Dear Lord, thank You for the opportunity to take my hurts and questions to You and to hear Your wisdom. May I always be open for Your answers. Amen.

Reflection

All Things

"And we know that for those who love God all things work together for good, for those who are called according to his purpose."

Romans 8: 28 – 29

I can't believe God let my nervous system start mis-firing and now I have to live with an essential tremor, or allowed Alzheimer's to take my mother away from her adoring family so I had to deal with all sorts of unexpected and unwanted changes. However, I am humbly grateful that he let me watch my children mature to adulthood with families of their own so now I can enjoy them as adults and that I found a congenial retirement village in which to live.

In Romans I am told that all things – good, bad and horrible – go into making me the person I am. That when I try, no matter my circumstances, to live in harmony with God's own will, I will be fitting into His plan for me. By faith I am told I am accepted just as I am – warts and all. I am what I am and what I am is wonderful in his sight!

O God, Creator of all, thank You for making me a part of Your magnificent plan. Teach me to wait patiently and confidently trusting you will show me my path. Amen

Reflection

Questions

"Why are you cast down, O my soul?
And why are you in turmoil within me?
Hope in God; For I shall praise Him,
My salvation and my God."

Psalm 42

Sometimes I get blue, feel unimportant. I used-to-be hostess at parties, deliver meals-on-wheels, help in the soup kitchen, run and play with my children, enjoy the companionship of singing in the choir – carols or Christian marching tunes. Surely there is still something at which I can succeed. Now my energy level is low, my voice quakes, and I wonder of what use I am to anyone, including the Lord. Then I read Psalm 42 and realize that when I persevere in doing the will of God, I will show His power in a person who perseveres, whatever the age. That's where I can now succeed.

I'm sure that there will be more times when I feel sad and inconsequential; when I ask, "Why??" I know, too, that the

Lord plans to give me more character-building situations. He will fine-tune my circumstances so that my character will finally succeed – that's His will.

Heavenly Father, I turn to You in prayer when I feel frustrated and unimportant; seeking, again, Your will for me. May I never stop hoping for Your abundant mercy or continuing to look to You for guidance. Amen.

Reflection

Fear

"The Lord is my light and my salvation; whom shall I fear? The Lord is the stronghold of my life; of whom shall I be afraid?"

Palm 27

It's the negative view of thinking that get me down. I fear getting weaker, being referred to as "tottering," "fragile," "ancient," or depending on others to do things for me. I am terrified of invasive medical tests or the thought of a drawn out illness or that my thinking becomes fossilized. When I focus on bad things that could happen, it paralyzes me from opening up to alternative possibilities. Then is when I turn to Psalm 27 and am reassured, again, that the Lord is with me as I seek a closer relationship with him.

Asking for help, seeking instructions on solving my problems, is the first phase. Waiting patiently for Him to answer is the harder second step. He will answer. By trusting, I gain more from difficult situations.

*Thank you, God, that you have given me the gift of long life and
a mission to fulfill. Help me to give up my negative thoughts of
aging and to know that Your grace is all I need. Amen.*

Reflection

What Purpose?

"Don't you know your body is a temple of the Holy Spirit within you, whom you have from God? You are not on your own, for you were bought with a price. So glorify God in your body.

1 Corinthians 6:19-20

A few days ago someone called and asked if I would talk to her mother about how I was managing my essential tremor. I was glad to pass along tips on living with shaking hands and voice. Several days later a friend called to ask what my secret was when dealing with lupus. We had lunch and chatted for a couple of hours. Then it dawned on me – I had had my prayers answered!

I had prayed asking why I'd been granted long life when I had such a disintegrating body. The answer came in opportunities to help others who had asked for the Lord's help with their problems. These acts of service were a way I can to be used to let God's love shine.

Holy Spirit, may Your light in me continue to shine as I travel through this phase of my journey. Amen.

Reflection

Anger

"If we live by the Sprit, let us also keep in step
with the Spirit."

Galatians 5:25

When I find myself fuming, incensed, furious, or angry at
something I think someone did or at my aging body, I am worn
out. It takes a lot of energy and time to carry on a big huff or
resentment! I have to keep reminding myself – over and over –
about each of the hurts, rehearsing/nursing again and again all
the reason I have to justify such feelings or actions. This takes a
lot of time; time taken away from enjoying my more pleasurable
pursuits.

Paul, in his letter to the Galatians, reminds me that there is
another way. When I ask for and listen to the guidance of the
Holy Spirit, who was sent by Christ especially for me, I'll be able

to let go all these negative feelings. With tutoring, I can enjoy the fruits of the Spirit and follow the plan laid out for me.

Heavenly Father, help me never to forget to trust my whole life to the guidance and influence of the Spirit. Amen.

Reflection

Be Still

"(Jesus) awake and rebuked the wind and he said
to the sea, "Peace! Be still!" and the wind ceased,
and there was a great calm. He said to them,
"Why are you so afraid? Have you still no faith?""

Mark 4:39-40

I took my credit card out of my wallet to make an online
purchase and forgot to return it, so I had no way to pay for the
department store purchase a few hours later. I can't find one
of the six pairs of "reading" glasses to read the newspaper. I
forgot to get new batteries for my hearing aid. I am frustrated
at my lack of recalling words for my cross word puzzle. My
grandson has not returned my call of two days ago. One of my
pill cylinders spilled all over the bathroom floor - how will I find
them without my glasses?

When my thoughts are whirling around and dark clouds of
frustration or dissatisfaction begin to swamp me, I struggle
to take a deep breath and remember Mark 4. Jesus calms the

waters then asks the disciples about their commitment to faith. Why am I fretting? I am in kept alive of my Savior so all I need to do is take a deep breath, ask for help and be still, believing the Holy Spirit will give the answer in some way.

Majestic God, calm the storms that rage in my life and let me experience Your peace. Amen.

Reflection

Shame

"For we know that the law is spiritual, but I am of the flesh, sold under sin. For I do not understand my own actions. For I do not do what I want, but I do the very thing I hate ..... I myself serve the law of God with my mind, but with my flesh I serve the law of sin."

Romans 7:15-25

When I remember the times I said nothing when someone was belittling another person, or making racial slurs, or passing on hurtful gossip, or when I even take part in cruel gossip, I feel ashamed. I know better than to do these things. I should have stopped such talk or reported the incident to the proper authority, but instead I said nothing. I usually feel guilty later and wonder why I let myself go along with the group. Then there are the times when I know what I should do, but choosing another way will get to close the situation sooner – and I live to regret not making the choice that I knew was the right one at the time.

In my repentance, I go to prayer. I know that the Holy Spirit knows my nature and suffers with me when I make bad choices. The Spirit is also always willing to give me guidance so I will be able to follow the thoughts of my new nature in Christ and to resist falling captive to my old nature.

Merciful God, forgive my stumbles in learning to walk in Your ways. Grant me strength to seek Your way in responding to temptations. Amen.

Reflection

All Alone

"Teach me to do your will, for you are my God.
Let Your good spirit lead me on a level path."

Psalm 143: 8

My family and my friends have not forgotten me, but sometimes it seems that way. It seems that everyone has things to do, places to go. And I am at the bottom of their to-do list – almost out-of-sight bottom. I am grateful for my lovely family and I know they have not forgotten me and they have good intentions about including me in activities, but their lives are crowded with civic activities and work related obligations. I understand. I do. I know I have not been abandoned, that they love me. And yet, at times I feel like a piece of fine china, put on a shelf only to be taken out on special days. I am grateful that God does not think of me as a treasure to be admired only on special days. He knows my feeble frame and loves me still. I can, at any time, bring my concerns to him and he will give me guidance. And when I am lonely perhaps I should call a friend and have a telephone chat or invite someone over to have a cookie and coffee. When I initiate contacts I am encouraging people to share in my life.

Heavenly Father, I do rejoice that You are near. Help me to reach out to others who may be having the same feelings of loneliness I am having today. In Jesus name I pray. Amen.

Reflection

Hopeless

"We can rejoice, too, when we run into problems and trials for we know that they are good for us – they help us to learn to be patient. And patience develops strength in character in us and helps us trust God more each time we use it until finally our hope and faith are strong and steady."

Romans 8:3-4

Impossible. That's how I feel sometimes about my situation. Just when I get my medication working, something changes and I need a different dose or need a change altogether; or when I think my finances are all straighten, something changes; or my glasses need changed, or teeth need a new procedure. I don't like being always in the state of change. I am in the degenerating generation and I wonder if I can be helped or my situation improved. I know that my doctors and care givers are doing the best for me, but I can't help questioning my circumstance.

In Romans Paul explains a lot to me. I am assured that all of God's children face problems now and then. That by following the guidance of the Holy Spirit – the helper the Lord gives us – we will be able to manage our challenges. I will learn patience, trust God's plan for me more, and grow in my faith.

Holy Spirit, help me make the decisions that show I am trusting the way God is leading me, even when I feel uncertain about the future. Amen.

Reflection

Joyful Noise

"Sing to the Lord a new song! For he has done marvelous things!
His right hand and his holy arm have worked salvation for him.
Make a joyful noise before the king, the Lord!"

Psalm 98: 1,6

I love to sing hymns! The marching ones, "Onward Christian Soldiers," "A Mighty Fortress ..." make my feet start tapping and arms swinging. The ones of praise, "Glory be to the Father," "The Old Rugged Cross," make my heart swell with thanksgiving. All the hymns we sing at Christmas are favorites, too. Of course, I can't march or dance to these tunes now, I can't even sing out loud. My arthritic knees only let me tap out the beats and my quaking voice is not only off-key, but an embarrassment for me (and all around me!). So I sing with my heart, mouthing the words silently with the sure knowledge that the Lord hears my praises even if people cannot.

I was delighted when my church changed hymn books – "up graded" to include modern tunes and words – and gave the old ones to anyone who wanted them. I keep one on my bedside table and sometimes at night have a hymn sing-a-long for one. It's much better to have the words in front of me instead of trying to remember the verses. My "remember-er" often gets words and tunes mixed up and I "sing a new song"!

Thank you, Lord, for hearing my full heart sing joyfully of Your wonders with praise even with my voice quakes. In Jesus name I pray. Amen

Reflection

Prejudice

"Then Peter began and said, "Now I really understand that God shows no partiality, but in every nation anyone who fears Him and does what is right is acceptable to Him."

Acts 10: 34,35

God shows no partiality, but sometimes I do. The other day, when I was driving my car, my front tire blew out. I pulled over to the side of the highway and called AAA. In a few minutes a rap on the window made me look up. There was a young man on a motor scooter with tattoos on both arms asking me if I was alright. Yes, I replied, not rolling down the window and making sure the door was locked. He smiled and said if I would open the trunk he would change the tire. I said, OK although I knew AAA would eventually rescue me. I pressed the trunk button and soon the tire was changed. That tattooed, scuffed bearded young man did not kidnap or rape me nor would he accept any money for his services! He just smiled and said he hoped someone would be as kind to his grandmother if she had problems and zoomed on his way.

I hold onto the opinions that are without just grounds. Kale, for example, that dark green, leathery, curly stuff, is an example having an opinion without just grounds. My daughter made a Kale smoothie and said, try it, you'll like it and it's full of nutrients. "Ugh," I said. "Just close your eyes and drink ... its good!" she said. It was good and I drank the whole thing and felt good afterward.

Heavenly Father, teach me to reserve judgement about things and people that are different or new to me. Give me an open mind and heart to listen to other opinions. Amen.

Reflection

Determination

"So, whatever it takes, I will be one who lives in the newness of life of those who are alive from the dead. I don't mean to say I am perfect. I haven't learned all I should even yet, but I keep working toward that day when I will finally be all that Christ saved me for and wants me to be."

Philippians 3: 11, 12

Paul is speaking to me here showing the way to live with these years I have been gifted. Despite my weakening physical condition, there are new areas of being a Christian I can explore. I can't let unfulfilled wants of yesterday govern how I act today as a senior saint. I may not have the stamina to serve at the soup kitchen or go on mission trips to far off place; but I can still serve here. I can keep up with current events, telephone or write a note to those who are ill or in distress. I can smile, share a laugh, and have a ready joke for all that visit me. I can listen with a sympathetic ear to those who are unhappy. I can keep in touch with far flung family members learning about their wishes, dreams, and "bucket lists," thus becoming more a part of their lives. I may be able to send someone some money to help with school expenses.

I believe the point Paul is making here is that, no matter your age, live in today and look forward to tomorrow. I'll always cherish the good memories of yesterday, but I look forward to being all I can at this time of life.

Lord, I am grateful for Your letting me be in the place I am. Keep me from bemoaning the things I do not have. Amen

Reflection

Remembrance

'"But the Helper, the Holy Spirit, whom the Father will send in my name, he will teach you all the things and bring to your remembrance all I have said to you."

John 14:26

I get confused and bewildered at all the TV options presented and sometimes have a hard time retrieving my favorite shows. I've learned to write down all of my doctor, dentist, and church appointments on my calendar. I am so grateful for my long-time friends and the new friends who are my age! They remember with me times of 'yesteryear' or things that happen during those years. There are many times, now, that I can't think of the name of a place and a friend will know. We older people help each other out when we are uncertain what to do or don't understand something clearly. We just think of such kindness as part of helping each other, it's a part of growing older together.

In the passage from John, Jesus explains to his audience, and to us, that they do not have to have instant recall of everything he has taught. There is a Helper, the Holy Spirit, whom the Farther will send. Maybe that help will be a friend or someone else who will help us out of our confusion.

Thank you, Holy Spirit, for teaching me to know of Your faithfulness and presence in my life and the world, even when my body fails me. Amen

Reflection

Asking

"For now we see through a glass, dimly, but then face to face. Now I know in part; then I shall know fully, even as I have been fully known."

1 Corinthians 13:12

Sometimes I don't see 'the big picture' of a situation in which I am involved; I only see what is immediately in front of me, therefore, I ask for solutions that are not at all right. The situation with my sister is a prime example: my younger sister is a stubborn, opinionated person, and I was often frustrated with our conversations. I prayed about this state of affairs, asking that her ways might be changed; then, one day came the answer: 'Maybe it's *you* who needs an attitude readjustment.' Wow! Not what I expected. I took this guidance and looked inward and our relationship got a lot better.

There have been other times that I have earnestly prayed and gotten unexpected answers: 'have faith, trust me and know that you don't know the whole picture.' Of course I cannot fathom the mysteries of the Lord's ways and I believe in his love of me. I am now leaving room in my petitions to include 'not my will, but yours be done' and am open to heavenly guidance.

Heavenly Father, help me appreciate all opportunities for renewal. Help me to trust the whole of my life to You and Your influence. Amen

Reflection

Fatigue

"I am weary with my moaning, every night I flood my bed with tears; I drench my couch with my weeping. ... The Lord has heard the sound of my weeping. The Lord has heard my plea; the Lord accepts my prayer."

Psalm 6:6, 8-9

I am exhausted with micro managing my medications, my doctor appointments and my limited lifestyle. Sometimes I get so confused about what-goes-where. It seems the negative thought of 'what-if' – I should fall and break a hip or back, I should get cancer, be put in a nursing home, have monumental medical bills – and the 'I-can't' overwhelms me. All I want is to keep my life on a steady level, to cut out all the waves; days when I feel good followed by days I struggle to get out of bed. My doctors tell me that having a wavy life goes along with my condition. I can accept that, but I need help in coping with these conditions. There are times I simply am unable to help myself. The solution is outside myself, above and beyond my abilities.

The Lord has heard me crying! He has listened to my requests and accepts my prayer for help. I need rescuing and I cannot do it myself. He is the source of everything I need.

Dear Lord, remind me that my suffering is only for a season, that your love endures forever. Give me strength for the faith journey ahead, just as You have before. Amen

Reflection

Prayer

"You can get anything – *anything* you ask for in prayer – if you believe."

Matthew 21:22

Jesus gives me the example of how to pray by the Lord's Prayer and Matthew assures me that I can get "anything" I ask for if I have faith, but that is not the end of the prayer story. No one mentions the length of human time it will take to be granted an answer – thirty minutes or 3-9 years or longer - nor in what form the answer will come – from a tweet, a chance encounter, a loving hug, direct word from the Holy Spirit. That's where faith comes into play. My prayer will be answered on his schedule and in his way.

Another adage is, "be careful what you pray for" and I can give an example. A few years back, I, in frustration, prayed "Lord, please give me the gift of patience!" He did. I continued to have multiple ways I needed to practice (and learn) the art of being patient. I learned to use and develop my God given skills and abilities to state of mind circumstances with a calmer state of mind instead of a fiery one.

Omniscient God, thank You for looking out for my best interests, even when I may not realize it. Amen.

Reflection

Anxiety

"Don't be anxious about anything; rather, bring up all of your requests to God in your prayers and partitions, along with giving thanks. Then the peace of God that exceeds all understanding will keep your hearts and minds safe in Christ Jesus."

Philippians 4:6-7

It's hard for me to follow this passage when I have 'lost' my car keys and am due at the doctor's office in thirty minutes. I do give thanks that I had no major repairs on the car this year. Or when I receive a nighttime call that a grandchild has been in a car accident; a friend confides her marriage is on the rocks; the Radiology Clinic calls to say my mammogram X-ray needs a retake. The list goes on about ways that can cause me concern or cause me to doubt my capacity to cope.

In Philippians I see a way out of this overwhelming sense of apprehension and fear: I can take my concerns and fears to God in prayer. When I make this effort and give thanks that he will listen, then I will receive the "peace of God that exceeds all understanding and will keep my heart and mind safe in Christ Jesus."

Holy and loving God, thank You for giving us mortals a way to deal with the anxiousness that we experience in our daily lives here on earth. Amen.

Reflection

Rejection

"This poor man cried, and the Lord heard him
and saved his out of all his troubles. The angel
of the Lord encamps around those that fear him,
and delivers them. .... Taste and see how good the
Lord is!"

Psalm 34: 6-8

All hurts and stings of rejection bring suffering to the intended
victim. Some are common, life experiences for older people like
snubbing: someone I know walks by and refuses to acknowledge
me – I feel rejected and am hurt. When I refuse to hear or
admit to another viewpoint beside my own, I am rejecting that
person's ideas. If I were to admit my ailing elderly parent in a
nursing home and never visit them, expecting Medicaid to take
care of their bills for the remainder of their lives, that is family
rejection. And, of course, the larger rejection topic brings in
the race issue: how I treat or relate to others that are not my
race, gender, or religion. No matter the circumstance, a rejected
person is suffering.

The Psalmist assures me that the sufferer is heard by the Lord. I am promised the Holy Spirit, God's messenger, will protect me when I cry out. God will protect and deliver all those who honor him.

Lord, forgive me when I offend someone. Where there is suffering help me to tend and to heal. Amen.

Reflection

Aching Bones – Slow Steps

"In the day of prosperity be joyful, and in the day of adversity consider: God has made the one as well as the other."

Ecclesiastes 7:14

This body of mine has served me well for 85 years. We have had many adventures: flying across the lake water skiing, jumping up and down cheering grandsons on the soccer field or basketball courts, two marriages, birthing four babies, several operations, and the cancerous stomach removed. The list can go on: fun times, sad times, and times of just enduring. It's been quite a ride but now is the time I need to honor this old friend by taking care of its physical needs. Instead of complaining about the things I can't do – the 'I used to' – I need to agree it's time to slow down.

God has promised me, as his child, that even in my elderly, earthly years I am of value. Although I cannot serve him with activities as I did in my younger years, I can still serve him in different ways. When I am willing to be of service he will show me what he needs me to do. Even if I do have arthritic joints and a slow step.

Heavenly Father, thank You for these extra years to learn more about and serve You in special ways. Amen.

Reflection

Joy

"This is the day the Lord has made, let us rejoice
and be glad in it.
O give thanks to the Lord, for he is good, for his
steadfast love endures forever."

Psalm 118:24, 29

I usually rejoice when I get out of bed that the Lord has given
me another day. I don't make a joyful noise or jump up and
down with joy, after all I am Presbyterian, but I do try to live a
joy-filled life. I give thanks that I am blessed with a new day, a
family who loves me, and friends I can count on. I know there
will be other days when my joints ache, my energy level is so
low I don't want to get out of bed – 'slow days,' days I need
more rest – they come with my astonishing number of years.
"Weeping may linger for the night, but joy comes with the
morning" (Psalm 30:5b).

I will have 'slow days,' but I know I am not alone. God is
with me, assuring me, calling for praise and encouraging me to

nurture his joy that is within me. Someone said, "life will change without our permission. It's our attitude that will determine the ride."

Heavenly Father, thank You for Your loving care. I praise You for giving me extra days to rejoice in Your love. Amen

Reflection

Living Life Now

"The righteous flourish like the palm tree, and grow like a cedar in Lebanon. They are planted in the house of the Lord; they flourish in the courts of God. They still bear fruit in old age; they are ever full of sap and green, to declare that the Lord is upright."

Psalm 92:12-15

I hope I can be like the 'righteous' mentioned in this Psalm. I hope that my heart will always be youthful though my body is not, and that I will find ways to live life today. There are ways of achieving this dream with joy because of my partnership with the Holy Spirit. I will be shown new ways to see familiar situations, given inner strength to give up 'the old way of doing things' and try the new. I hope to be ever growing and expanding in my faith journey. I will find something new to learn every day – a new bird or flower, meet a new friend, hear of someone's fresh adventure, find a different book – and I will laugh every day. I will smile at all I meet, even when my old bones ache, and tell my family how much I love them. I will take time to appreciate the beauty of the world the Lord created and that surrounds me every day – the majestic, ever changing cloud formations, the beauty of the shadows slowly moving across the landscape as the sun passes, the butterflies flitting from here to there.

Holy Spirit, help me live today by bearing Your fruit and being a good manager of the gifts given to me. Amen.

Reflection

Kindness

"Be kind to each other, tenderhearted, forgiving one another, just as God has forgiven you because you belong to Christ."

Ephesians 4:32

"Don't you realize how patient (God) is being with you? Or don't you care? Can't you see that he has been waiting all this time without punishing you, to give you time to turn from your sin? His kindness is meant to lead you to repentance."

Roman 2:4

Many times people have asked me for a favor – small, as in helping reach for an item on a grocery store shelf, holding the door open for a mother with a stroller; larger, returning a book to the library when I am returning mine – and I am happy to oblige. Or I don't mind picking up someone's paper from the yard when they are out of town. These random acts of kindness are second nature to me. My problem comes when I hear someone say racists remarks or curse a child, animal, or another person when a simple act of open-mindedness would have been better. This is not my sin, but it stills hurts me.

Paul reminds the Romans (and me) that God sees all. He is patient wanting us to be kind to one another just as he is kind to us. However, God also does not forget. He remembers all our unkindness's and there will be a judgment someday.

Gracious God, help me to follow Jesus' example of loving servanthood. Amen.

Reflection

Live Gratefully!

"Let them thank the Lord for his steadfast love,
for his wondrous works to the children of man!
For he satisfies the longing soul, and the hungry
soul he fills with good things."

Psalm 107:8-9

I often start or my end my day by listing five things for which
I am thankful or grateful. The thankful list can run something
like this: I live in the USA (more particularly in Alabama), I
have a healthy family who love me, I have lived long enough to
see my children into adulthood, my grandchildren to maturity,
and to hold a great-grandchild, I still drive a car, I have caring
medical personnel. All these things have to do with my human
nature. The grateful list has more to do with the divine: I have
a God who loves me (even though he knows my frame), I have a
Savior who redeems me and teaches me the way I should live, I
have a Holy Spirit who walks with me every hour of my journey,
I have God's written word, and I have fellow church members
with whom I can study the Lord's word.

Looking over my 'thankful' and my 'grateful' list each day, I cannot help but be humble. I shall give thanks for these graces by living gratefully!

Merciful God, as I live in this mortal world I am humbled by the love and graces You show me every day. May I never grow too old to grow in gratitude. Amen.

Reflection

Death

"Because of the tender mercy of our God, whereby the sunrise shall visit us from on high to give light to those who sit in darkness and in the shadow of death, to guide our feet into the way of peace."

Luke 1:78 -79

I take comfort in this speech by Zacharias telling of the coming of Christ Jesus. I, too, have sat in darkness when a loved one died. In my long life span I have been to many funerals: my parents, my husband, many relatives, and friends. Death is another phase of life, I know and accept this, but the loss of someone close leaves a big hole in my life when they are gone. I have sat in that darkness, not wondering where the loved one had gone or 'why now?', but wondering how I was going to cope with a big ache in my life. Even though I have great memories to comfort me, the way forward seems so murky and filled with uncertainties when death comes. Into this darkness comes Zacharias' message and promise: God will send a guide who will set my feet "into the way of peace." That peace is 'the peace of

God' which passes all human understanding. I will claim this promise through prayer and trust. It may take a while, but the Lord always fulfils his promises.

Dear Jesus, light of the world, I humbly thank You for guiding my feet in times when I feel in the shadows on my journey of life and for leading me to peace. Amen.

Reflection

Devotions And Texts

Printed in the United States
By Bookmasters